Introduction to EARTH'S RESOURCES

WHY AIR IS IMPORTANT

Kelly Spence

Crabtree Publishing Company

www.crabtreebooks.com

Crabtree Publishing Company
www.crabtreebooks.com

Author: Kelly Spence
Editorial Director: Kathy Middleton
Editor: Ellen Rodger
Picture Manager: Sophie Mortimer
Design Manager: Keith Davis
Children's Publisher: Anne O'Daly
Proofreader: Debbie Greenberg
Production coordinator and
  Prepress technician: Ken Wright
Print coordinator: Katherine Berti

Library and Achives Canada Cataloguing in Publication

Title: Why air is important / Kelly Spence.
Names: Spence, Kelly, author.
Description: Series statement: Introduction to Earth's resources | Includes bibliographical references and index.
Identifiers: Canadiana (print) 20200284592 | Canadiana (ebook) 20200284622 | ISBN 9780778782001 (softcover) | ISBN 9780778781868 (hardcover) | ISBN 9781427126047 (HTML)
Subjects: LCSH: Air—Juvenile literature.
Classification: LCC QC161.2 .S64 2020 | DDC j533/.6—dc23

Library of Congress Cataloging-in-Publication Data

Names: Spence, Kelly, author.
Title: Why air is important / Kelly Spence.
Description: St. Catharines, ON ; New York : Crabtree Publishing Company, 2021. | Series: Introduction to earth's resources | Includes index.
Identifiers: LCCN 2020029734 (print) | LCCN 2020029735 (ebook) | ISBN 9780778781868 (hardcover) | ISBN 9780778782001 (paperback) | ISBN 9781427126047 (ebook)
Subjects: LCSH: Air--Juvenile literature.
Classification: LCC QC161.2 .S68 2021 (print) | LCC QC161.2 (ebook) | DDC 551.5--dc23
LC record available at https://lccn.loc.gov/2020029734
LC ebook record available at https://lccn.loc.gov/2020029735

Crabtree Publishing Company

www.crabtreebooks.com   1-800-387-7650

Published in 2021 by Crabtree Publishing Company

Copyright © Brown Bear Books Ltd 2020

Published in Canada
Crabtree Publishing
616 Welland Ave.
St. Catharines, ON
L2M 5V6

Published in the United States
Crabtree Publishing
347 Fifth Ave
Suite 1402-145
New York, NY 10016

Printed in the U.S.A./082020/CG20200710

In Canada: We acknowledge the financial support of the Government of Canada through the Canada Book Fund for our publishing activities.

Contents

What Is Air?

Air is all around. It moves through our bodies, fills every place we go, and surrounds Earth. Without air, life would not exist.

Air is a mixture of different gases. A gas is something that has no fixed shape. It will expand, or get bigger, to fill any space. The different gases in the air are made up of tiny **particles**. Air becomes dirty, or **polluted**, when harmful substances are added to it. Air pollution is bad for our health and the environment.

Aerosol sprays are used for household cleaners and air fresheners.

Air is about 78% **nitrogen**, 21% **oxygen**, and 1% other gases (including **carbon dioxide)**.

You cannot see air or feel it, but it is all around us.

Aerosols

Tiny materials **suspended** in the air are called aerosols. Aerosols can be natural or human-made. They can be solid or liquid. Natural aerosols include sea salt and dust. Aerosols made by humans include smoke and **pollutants**. Most aerosols are too small to see. The smaller and lighter an aerosol is, the longer it stays in the air. Some aerosols last for days. Some even float around for years.

A single aerosol particle can be 1/1,000 the width of a human hair!

Air and Plants

Plants provide oxygen, which is essential for almost all living things to survive.

Plants use water, sunlight, and a gas called carbon dioxide to make their own food. This process is called photosynthesis. A plant soaks up water through its roots. The water travels through the plant to its leaves. The leaves absorb sunlight and carbon dioxide. The **carbon** and oxygen are separated. The plant uses the carbon to grow. It releases the oxygen back into the air.

Plants make the oxygen that we breathe.

One tree can absorb **48 pounds** (22 kg) of carbon dioxide each year.

Tiny plants called phytoplankton produce **50%** of the oxygen in the world.

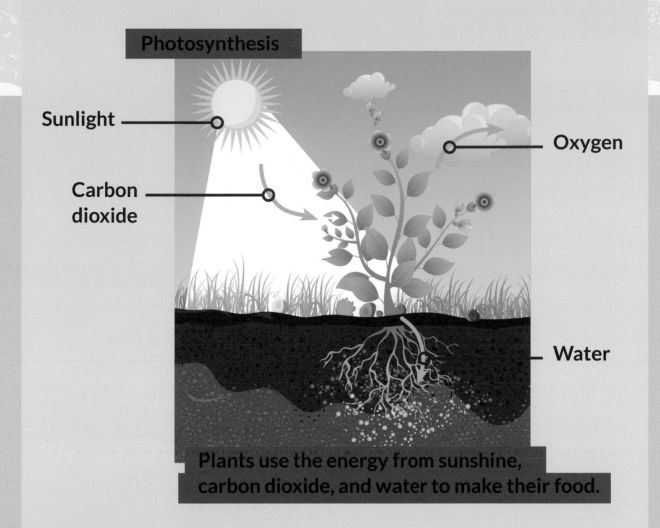

Photosynthesis

Sunlight

Oxygen

Carbon dioxide

Water

Plants use the energy from sunshine, carbon dioxide, and water to make their food.

Cleaning the Air

Plants don't only provide oxygen for us to breathe. They also help clean the air. Plants use carbon dioxide to make their food. At the same time, they take in and break down other gases. This removes pollutants from the air. They also trap pollutants on their leaves.

Air and the Human Body

Take a deep breath and feel your lungs fill with air!

The process of breathing is called respiration. When you breathe in through your nose or mouth, air flows into your lungs. In your lungs, oxygen passes into your blood. Oxygen travels to other parts of your body through your blood. The oxygen combines with other **elements** to give your body the energy to grow and move.

The longest a person has held their breath is 22 minutes and 22 seconds!

Oxygen makes up about **two-thirds** of the human body.

Breathe Out

Carbon dioxide (or CO_2) is a waste product in the human body. This means the body does not use it. CO_2 travels through the blood back to the lungs. The CO_2 is released when you breathe out. Plants use the CO_2 we and other animals breathe out to make their food. This is part of the **oxygen cycle**.

A person takes about **22,000 breaths** every day.

When we exercise, our bodies need more oxygen.

Moving Air

Wind is created by moving air. Wind dries our clothes, affects the weather, and helps plants grow.

During the day, sunlight heats the ground. Air near the ground warms up too. When air heats up, the air particles speed up and spread out. The air becomes lighter and rises. This makes space for cooler, heavier air to move in below. This movement creates wind.

Wind speed is measured on the Beaufort scale. This goes from 0 to 12. The strongest winds come with hurricanes.

Hurricane force winds are at **12** on the Beaufort scale. This can destroy buildings.

The strongest winds in a hurricane reach **155 miles per hour** (250 km/h).

A windsurfer uses the wind to move across the water.

Wind Power

Wind carries heat and moisture around the world. It also moves dust and pollution. Some plants rely on the wind to help them grow because the wind carries pollen and seeds. Wind can be as gentle as a light breeze or strong enough to power sailing boats. The strongest winds come with hurricanes and tornadoes. They can damage trees, cars, and houses.

The Atmosphere

Earth is surrounded by a layer of gases called the atmosphere. It acts like a shell that protects the planet.

The atmosphere has five layers. The layers become thinner and warmer as you move away from Earth. The troposphere is the closest layer. It rises about 6 miles (10 km) above Earth's surface. Most weather happens in the troposphere.

Atmosphere

The atmosphere is about 300 miles (480 km) thick.

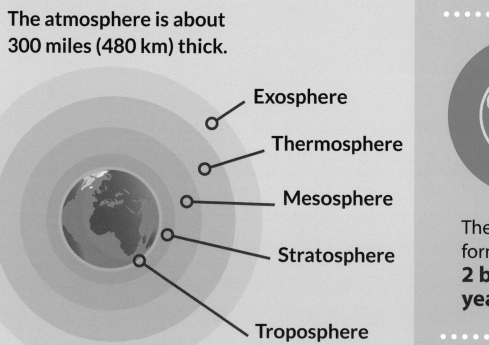

Exosphere

Thermosphere

Mesosphere

Stratosphere

Troposphere

The ozone layer formed about **2 billion years** ago.

The Ozone Layer

The ozone layer is an important part of the upper atmosphere. The Sun sends out powerful rays that contain **ultraviolet** (UV) light. Too much UV light can cause sunburns and health problems, such as skin cancer. The ozone layer protects people by absorbing these harmful rays.

The ozone layer absorbs about 98% of UV rays.

Wear sunscreen to protect your skin from the Sun.

The Greenhouse Effect

Life exists on Earth because our planet is the right temperature.

Earth is the only planet in our solar system that supports life. This is thanks to its atmosphere. During the day, the atmosphere stops the Sun from heating Earth too much. At night, the gases in the atmosphere trap heat and hold it close to the planet's surface. This helps Earth stay at the right temperature. It is called the greenhouse effect.

Earth would freeze without the greenhouse effect.

Without the greenhouse effect, Earth would be **0 °F (-18 °C).**

The Sun is **93 million miles** (150 million km) from Earth.

Earth's atmosphere traps some of the Sun's heat, which warms the planet.

Livestock such as cows give out methane, which is a greenhouse gas.

Greenhouse Gases

Gases that trap the Sun's heat are called **greenhouse gases**. Water vapor, carbon dioxide, methane, and nitrous oxide are greenhouse gases. Greenhouse gases come from natural and human-made sources. Methane is released from landfills, or dumps, and from livestock. Nitrous oxide is released by farming practices. Pollution created by humans has made new gases that also heat up Earth.

Where Does Pollution Come From?

We know pollution is harmful, but where does it come from?

Some pollution comes from natural sources, but most air pollution is created by humans. People burn **fossil fuels** in cars, airplanes, and power plants. **Emissions** from these activities pollute the air. CO_2 created by these human activities is also increasing the heat from the greenhouse effect.

Smoke from volcanoes is a natural source of pollution.

Nine out of **ten** people in the world breathe polluted air.

Volcanoes produce about **200 million tons** (180 million metric tons) of CO_2 each year.

Waste gases from cars help to make ozone.

Bad Ozone

Up high, ozone is helpful, but it is dangerous near the ground. Ozone at ground level is created on sunny days by a chemical reaction between some kinds of pollutants. There is more ground-level ozone when it is hot outside. Breathing in ozone is like getting a sunburn in your lungs.

Cars and industry produce about **24 billion tons** (22 billion metric tons) of CO_2 each year.

Climate Change

One of the biggest impacts of air pollution is climate change.

Earth has warmed up and cooled down many times over millions of years. This is called climate change. Air pollution from humans over the past 150 years has made the planet's temperature rise much faster. When we burn fossil fuels, extra greenhouse gases become trapped in the atmosphere. The heat absorbed by these extra gases causes the temperature on Earth to increase.

Climate change is making deadly wildfires more common. In late 2019 and early 2020, wildfires raged across Australia.

25.5 million acres (10 million hectares) were burned.

More than **1 billion** animals died.

Around **3,000** homes were destroyed.

Effects of Climate Change

Warmer temperatures are causing polar ice caps to melt quickly. Water in the oceans is heating up and expanding. All this extra water has raised sea levels, which covers more land and floods coastal areas. Climate change could lead to more extreme weather in the future.

Warmer temperatures are melting the ice at the South Pole.

Harmful to Health

Pollution isn't just bad for the environment. It is also harmful to human health. It can even be deadly.

Being around polluted air for a little while can hurt your eyes and make you cough and sneeze. If you are around polluted air for a long time, it can cause serious health problems. Bad air can damage your lungs, cause **asthma**, and lead to other diseases such as cancer. People who live near industrial sites or in busy cities have a higher chance of getting sick.

This girl takes medicine from an inhaler to help ease her asthma.

Air pollution causes **seven million** deaths each year.

An app on a smartphone shows the air pollution level each day.

The Air Quality Index (AQI) measures how polluted the air is. Different colors tell people whether it is safe to breathe the air outside.

 Green – good

 Yellow – moderate (not very good or very bad)

 Orange – unhealthy for certain people, such as the elderly or children

 Red – unhealthy

 Purple – very unhealthy

 Dark red – hazardous (everyone might have health problems)

Indoor Air Pollution

Air pollution isn't just a problem outside. It can be even more harmful inside.

People spend about 90 percent of their time indoors. Pollution levels can be higher inside than outside. Cigarette smoke, mold, and chemicals from household cleaners are indoor air pollutants. Breathing unclean air is especially bad for older people and children. It can cause dizziness, headaches, shortness of breath, and more serious health problems.

Black mold comes from damp air, a leaking pipe, or rainwater.

Indoor pollution can be **10 times** worse than outdoor pollution.

3.8 million people die each year from indoor air pollution.

Black mold is a dangerous indoor pollutant.

Air purifiers can help to remove pollutants from the air inside a house.

Removing Indoor Pollutants

Ventilation (a way of providing fresh air) is important to stop pollutants from collecting together. Opening a window is an easy way to allow air to move around. Some people also use air purifiers to remove particles and gases. These machines suck in air and capture particles on a filter, then push the clean air back into the room.

Wind Power

Windmills were used for hundreds of years to grind grain and pump water.

Wind is a clean, or non-polluting, **renewable** source of energy. Today, wind **turbines** are used to make electricity. A number of wind turbines can be grouped together to make a wind farm. Wind farms are often built on the water to capture strong winds offshore. By 2050, one-third of the world's energy may come from wind turbines.

The United Kingdom's Walney Extension is one of the world's largest offshore wind farms.

This wind farm covers **56 square miles** (145 square km).

It can produce enough electricity to power nearly **600,000** homes.

Each of the turbines at the Walney Extension is 623 feet (190 m) tall.

Electricity from the Wind

The wind makes the blades on the wind turbine spin around. The blades are attached to a long rod called a shaft. When the blades spin, the shaft rotates, or turns. The spinning shaft powers a **generator** that makes electricity. The electricity is sent through cables, or power lines, to bring power to homes, schools, and other buildings.

Wind turbines use large blades to catch the power of the wind.

Working Together

**Everyone on Earth shares the air.
We must work together to keep it clean.**

Many countries and cities have rules about how much pollution a company can produce. If the company makes too much pollution, it has to pay a fine. Other places reward people and companies that make environmentally friendly choices. Electric cars run on batteries. They do not produce CO_2. In the city of Oslo, in Norway, people who buy electric cars can park in city-owned lots for free.

These cars are recharging their batteries.

 China wants to have **70%** of its electricity come from solar power by 2050.

 **99 percent** of cars in the United States burn gasoline, adding **1 billion tons** (0.9 billion metric tons) of CO_2 to the air each year.

Hydroelectricity uses the force of moving water to make electricity.

Air-Friendly Energy

Burning fossil fuels causes a lot of air pollution. The best way to reduce this kind of air pollution is to find other clean ways to make energy. Replacing power from fossil fuels with wind power prevents 200 million tons (180 million metric tons) of air pollution a year. Renewable energy sources such as wind, water, and sunlight make energy without polluting.

What Can I Do?

Here's a list of ideas to help keep the air clean. Talk to a parent or caregiver about small steps everyone in your family can take to do their part.

- Why not walk or ride your bike for short journeys instead of driving?

- For longer trips, take public transit or join with friends to carpool.

- Use less energy at home. Turn off electrical devices when you're done using them. Switch off the lights when you leave a room.

- If you have a garden, plant trees to help reduce pollution.

- Grow plants inside your home to help keep the air clean.

Quiz

How much have you learned about the air? It's time to test your knowledge!

1. What is the lowest level of the atmosphere called?

a) humanosphere

b) troposphere

c) life zone

2. What is air made of?

a) nitrogen, oxygen, and other gases

b) smoke and steam

c) smog and haze

3. Which greenhouse gas contributes the most to climate change?

a) carbon dioxide

b) wind

c) zinc

4. What does a wind turbine produce?

a) gasoline

b) ozone

c) electricity

5. What is the Air Quality Index?

a) a list of kinds of air pollution

b) a measure of how healthy the air is

c) how long pollution stays in the atmosphere

Answers on page 32.

Glossary

asthma A condition that affects a person's breathing . It can be made worse by air pollution.

carbon An element that is part of the human body

carbon dioxide (CO_2) A gas that is found naturally in the atmosphere, which is also produced when we burn fossil fuels

elements Substances that cannot be broken down into smaller substances

emissions Substances released into the air

fossil fuels Fuels formed in the earth from plants and animals that died millions of years ago

generator A machine that changes mechanical energy into electrical energy

greenhouse gases Gases that build up in the atmosphere and trap heat

nitrogen A gas that makes up most of the air

oxygen A gas that is found in air that animals need to breathe

oxygen cycle How oxygen travels through nature

particles Very small pieces

pollutants Substances that cause pollution

polluted Made dirty with waste

renewable Able to be replaced and will not run out

suspended Supported by something invisible

turbines Engines connected to blades turned by fluid or air

ultraviolet (UV) Powerful rays of light that are invisible

Find out More

Books

Ajmera, Maya. *Every Breath We Take: A Book About Air.* Charlesbridge, 2016.

Kopp, Megan. *Energy from Wind: Wind Farming* (Next Generation Energy). Crabtree Publishing, 2016.

London, Martha. *Looking Into the Atmosphere* (Looking at Layers). The Child's World, 2020.

Sawyer, Ava. *Humans and Earth's Atmosphere: What's in the Air?* Capstone Press, 2018.

Websites

https://breathelife2030.org/
This is the website of BreatheLife, a global campaign for clean air.

https://climatekids.nasa.gov/10-things-air/
Visit this website to discover ten interesting things about air.

https://climatekids.nasa.gov/air-pollution/
This NASA website looks at the causes of climate change.

https://spaceplace.nasa.gov/atmosphere/en/
Go to this website to find information about the atmosphere.

www.nationalgeographic.org/video/edu-wind-turbines/
Watch this video to see how wind turbines work.

Index

Quiz answers

1. b; 2. a; 3. a; 4. c; 5. b